GOD'S BLESSING PLANS

TO PROSPER YOU

Author: Willeen G. Williams

God's Blessing Plans

GOD' S BLESSING PLANS

TO PROSPER YOU

God's Blessing Plans

GOD'S BLESSING PLANS

TO PROSPER YOU

Author: Willeen Williams

The Alpha Word House Publisher

The Alpha Word House Publisher

Copyright ©2017 by Willeen G. Williams

Library of Congress Cataloging in- Publication Data

Washington, D.C.

God's Blessing Plans: To Prosper You   Author: Willeen G. Williams

ISBN- 978-0-9987241-4-0

Printed in the United States of American

GOD'S BLESSING PLANS

TO PROSPER YOU

Contents

God's Blessing Plans

GOD'S BLESSING PLANS

TO PROSPER YOU

Author: Willeen G. Williams

The Alpha Word House Publisher

God's Blessing Plans

Introduction

God always have the right plans for our life even when trouble may try to appear. The Lord will make away for us to escape the enemy trap. The love, God has for everyone greater than anyone could even think or believe on this earth. There is a blessing staying in the plans of God, and depending on the Lord with all your heart. God able to give us peace in the midst of every circumstance in our life. "These things I have spoken unto you, that in me ye might have peace" (KJV). God is saying, I promise you peace no matter what the problem may look like in your life.

.

God's Blessing Plans

Chapter -1

_____

What is a plan?

A plan is something an individual desire to do soon

without delay. A plan is something put together by an

individual, and desire to achieve at a certain time. There are

different types of plans people will use to reach their

destiny.

There is always something we like to do someday for

ourselves or love one. Plans are designed to be put into the

right perspective in life. Sometimes our ideas may take a

little time to get up off the ground.

The act of planning you need to think it out carefully, and

the plans of consideration getting done things right.

Example, a construction worker building a house for an

individual too own. The company must have a blue print

already laid out how the individual like for the home to be built.

It will take careful planning to build a house, and find the right type of material to complete the project. It is imperative to understand that it takes more than talking about building a house.

It will take skills, knowledge, money, and the right hired labors to finish the project. Example, planning a trip will take time finding the location you desire to visit, date, time, money, and others you may be planning to take on the trip with you.

It is essential to understand everything we do in life always connect to some type of planning. Every day we are thinking about what to do tomorrow. We may think about what type clothes, you plan to wear for work. We also a plan time for breakfast, and the time you may plan to leave home in the morning. Jesus should always be in our plan on the top of our list every day.

There good reason why we are here, and because it was already in God's plan. The Lord already had our destiny in mind. There is nothing in life done without a plan. Do you have a plan? It is important to have a plan in our life already in our hearts

"Commit thy works unto the Lord, and thy thoughts shall be established" (KJV). We should seek God concerning our plans to lead us in the right direction. God already knowns the directions we should take in life.

The Lord will allow us to walk right into our destiny, and fulfill our dreams. It is imperative to understand a life without no perception spells no future for the individual to hold on. "Where there is vision the people perish" (KJV). It is imperative to have a vision, and follow it. There is no doubt in my mind, and when God has given us a vision it imperative to follow, and according to the will of God.

It is essential to work your planning, and our vision together. It is important to do everything the right way God's plans. The process will take time, and putting things in the right perspective for our life to be completely develop. It is God's desire to see us bless with the right plans for our future. It is imperative for us to walk in God's plan today, and be bless of the Lord.

How Can a Natural Plan Work?

Yes, the natural plans it will sometimes work for us in life, and sometimes does not always work. Example we sometimes may plan to work on a job for 20-25 years, and something may not work out in your plan. Sometimes there are situations that could arrive in your life causing the individual not to work that long on that job. It is imperative to understand that God may have a different path for your life. We never know in life the directions might be changed for our good on the journey.

It is essential to try and understand things may change in our life, and it maybe the best for us. Life sometimes is filled with ups and downs along the way. Even though circumstances can change in a blink of an eye. God always holds our future in his hands, and no man or woman can change God's blue print for our life.

The natural plan we draw out sometimes for our life it seems so plan, and beautiful. God has an awesome way of showing us which plan, and the way it is going to work. Yes, God already knows the plans of the enemy, and know how to protect you from the enemy plans of action. The enemy always try to trap God's people destiny, and the plans of God is greater.

It is imperative to picture our life on a higher level, and God has another plan for our future. Sometimes life may seem to be a little complicated, and we try to find the right direction for ourselves. "For my thoughts are not your thoughts, neither are your ways my ways, saith the Lord" (KJV). You may have thought your past, and said these are my plans and no one can change my mind.

Even though we may have thought this is our plan, and may not be God's plan for your life. Have you asked yourself a question? Why things are not going the way I planned it? You may have asked, yourself these questions sometime in life. Why you, could not understand the reason things heading in another direction?

The devil had a plot, and God had the right plan. God already knows the right plan for our life. Example, my plan was not to attend college, and just roam into the sun set have fun, relax, travel a little in life. God already knew the best directions for me to travel in life.

God's Blessing Plans

It is imperative to understand God already plan our life even before being born on the earth. What we may have thought it does not really matters, and God knows what is best for us. The trick of the enemy will try to make you think this is the right plan for you. Example, you may have chosen to work in a manufacturing plant making ladies clothes.

These plants have a lot dust, and require some lifting in the work place. God's plan was getting us out of the plant, and working for a better company. God's plan is to place us in a large organization as a supervisor or CEO in a company. Sometimes, we have the desire to stay content in the same place, and God wants to elevate us to another level. We must praise, and worship God, and let God excel us to a new place in life.

The devil will try to stop God's people from receiving their blessing, and from staying in the will of God. The plans God has for our life is the correct plans. The enemy will try to make you think that is not right choice. "Where fore my beloved brethren, let every man be swift to hear, and slow to speak. slow to wrath" (KJV). It is imperative to listen to the voice of God in our life. It is important not to move fast, and wait on God.

Thought I Had the Right Plan

The plans that God has for our life is far more than anyone can ask or even think. The path that you might have supposed to taken went in another direction in your life. Life, sometimes have a lot of twist, and turns along our journey. I can remember in my experience trying to make plans for myself, and it did not workout according my plans.

My plans were to finish high, and that was going to be it for me. I can remember getting does dead end jobs, and it was not paying nothing but minimum wages. The pay check back in those days was very low trying to make ends

meet for me

I was not interested during that time going to college,

and in my mind just wanted a quick plan in life. I found

out the quick plan was not the right choice to make in life.

It was not easy heading down that road in life with nothing

to really keep me stable on my journey in life.

I just wanted to work, and have a good time. Yes, I was

very young, and didn't fully understand how things operate

in the real world. My feet got tested in the water, and I was

no longer sitting on the side of the bank.

Sometimes our love ones will try to encourage us to go

to college or military after finishing school. I thought my

plan was going to work on my time table. We sometimes

don't want to listen, and try to have our agenda. I was no

longer in high school, and grown on my own. My feet kept

getting tested in the water, and thinking I could handle life like a checker game.

We sometimes can miss our blessing by not listening to God speaking to us. I kept sitting with my feet in the water, and it was raising up closer to my waist. Example, "And he said come, And when Peter come down out of the ship, he walked on the water, to go to Jesus" (KJV). Yes, we sometimes know God is telling us to come on in this direction, and fail to hear the voice of God.

"But when he saw the wind boisterous, he was afraid and beginning to sink, he cried, saying Lord, save me" (KJV). We may keep letting our feet stay in the water, and we can't see the complete consequence of the matter.

Once, we began to see our plan is not working, and we almost drowning during the midst of the storm. We start crying out to God help me, and you about to sink please don't let my feet slip. Thought, I had the right plan for my life, and it didn't work out. God's plan is the right plan for our life.

God's Plan has total victory

It is imperative to know the plans of God, and the things the Lord have desired for us. Why does God's plan works the best for our life? We have always dreamed of an exciting life, and doing great things. God's desire is for us to serve him, and live a prosperous life.

Sometimes along the way we go through somethings in life it only makes us stronger. "For I know the thoughts that I think towards you saiths the Lord, thoughts of peace, and not of evil, and to give you expected end" (KJV). It is essential we try to understand that God loves us and desire the best for his people. It is imperative we stay in the plans of God, and don't try to use our ideas.

God always have the right plans for our life even when trouble may try to appear, and the Lord will make away for us to escape the enemy trap. The power of God will overthrow, any road blocks the devil try to set up against us.

"No weapon that is form against you shall prosper; and every tongue raise that shall raise against in judgement thou shalt condemn" (KJV). The enemy will keep trying to bring us down, and God's plan will always work out for good to bless us.

It is important to trust God, and we should never think our plan can work better than God's plan. The devil will sometime make you think God telling us to go this way. It is imperative to know the voice of the Lord. "The thief cometh not, but for to steal, and to kill and destroy" (KJV). The enemy has a plan as well to try to destroy the people of God's life. There is victory in God's plan.

It is imperative for us to understand the devil does not want people to live happy, and have the best things in life.

God's Blessing Plans

"I am come that they might have life, and that they might have it more abundantly" (KJV). God is letting us know come on get in the Master's plan.

The plan God wants to offer us is a better plan, and a life time benefits that will never run out. Example, we can work for a company and it will offer you three different plans for us to choose one. Sometimes the company will change their plans for the employees, and now we must pick another plan that year. The plans will not be the same as the other one we choice before on that job. God's plan is always better for us.

The plan God can offer us always stay the same, and we will never need to worry about it being a lapse in the plan. The plan God has for our life is everlasting joy that is unspeakable. God's plan is filled with love, peace, and understanding when no one else seems to know us. God will always know the right plan for his people that works.

God's Blessing Plans

It is imperative to stay in the will of God, and not our will for the life we choose to live. There is never failure in God, and nothing is impossible for the Lord to handle. My desire is to continue to follow God no matter how things may look in life.

It is essential to realize that somethings do not work out for a reason in our life. "And we know that all things work together for good to them that love God, to them who are called according to his purpose" (KJV). God already have a plan for us, and we must trust God at his word.

God is full of love, and wants the best for us all the time. There are things that happen to us, and we try to figure it all out. It is not always meant for us to guess a reason for that plan not working out for us. God will always know what is best for us even before we try to plan it in our mind. The plans of God are always better than our plans.

God's Blessing Plans

I can remember while in high school wanting to go in the
Navy Military. I was young, and was really excited about
going on that journey. The closer I was getting to finishing
high my mind began to change, and I wanted to do
something else different in life.

"For thoughts are not your thoughts, neither are your
ways my ways, Saith the Lord" (KJV). It does not matter
the things we think in our minds, and it is not always God's
plans for our life. God's plans there is victory.

We can sat back think about all the earthly desire in our,
and make a sketch of your life. It may not be in God's
plans for our life to go in that direction. "For as the heavens
are higher than the earth, so are my ways are higher than
your ways, and my thought than your thoughts" (KJV). Our
plans for our life was already in God's hands, and even
before we were born on this earth.

God's Blessing Plans

Have ever asked yourself a question in your mind? How can I plan a great future for the rest of my life? Yes, we have thought about trying to make things go a certain way in life. When the plan is not going our way, it tends make us upset. God's plans are always better for us in life. Sometimes we can't understand the outcome in the situation, and the reason.

God is an all seeing, and his eyes is in ever place. "The eyes of the Lord is in every place, beholding the evil and the good" (KJV). God will hold back the plans of the enemy that tries to destroy our life. The plans God have for our life is good, and the Lord desires the best for us in life.

God planned us even before the creation of the earth was even form. There is nothing too hard for God to do for us in his plan. Example, I had planned to meet a friend to the mall at 1:00 pm one day, and things didn't go according to our plans. The train had everyone held up, and the cars was caught up in a traffic stop for about two blocks.

God's Blessing Plans

After the train pass, through on the rail road tracks, and the traffic crossing there was a two-car wreck three blocks ahead of us. God already knew the situation ahead of time. I thank God for not allowing me to be in midst of that two - car accident on that day. The Lord has a reason for everything that happens in our life.

Yes, God had delayed my plans going to the mall. God had allowed the train to come, and to hold me up in the traffic. I believed God had stop me, and some other people from being involved in the wreck that day. Sometimes we may get upset cause things didn't go according to the way we planned it, and the Lord knows best for our life. There is victory in God's plans.

It is imperative to understand things does not always go the way we planned it. "A man's heart deviseth his way: but directed his steps" (KJV). God know every step we should take in our life. The Lord already knew the train was going to come through that day at that time. God always has a reason for things to work out on our behalf in life. God's plan is the best for us, and no other plan can over power the Lord's plans. There is victory in God's plans.

Life is filled with so many choices, and we sometimes think it is the right plan, and it is not the right one. God's plan is to prosper us and not to hurt us. We can't look at our life like a map, and you pull the information up on a GPS system.

God's directions for our life is much greater than we planned. We must trust God with the plans he designed for us to live. Let's allow God to make all the plans, and get out the way of the Lord's decisions for us to live.

We must continue to wait on God, and allow the Lord to direct our path. It is essential to understand when we go on our own path, and it will be the wrong direction to go in life. Example, you are planning to go New York, and you heading South toward Florida that is the wrong direction for your journey.

God will let us know this not the right place, and we should turn around to get back on the correct path. "Teaching to observe all things whatsoever I have commanded you: and lo, I am with you always even, unto the end of the world" (KJV). Even, when we have made the wrong turn in our life, and God has promised he never leave us alone in the wilderness by ourselves.

Sometimes we have friends that been in our life for several years promises to be there for us. Sometimes the plans do not always work out with some of the friends in your life. God's plan is the right choice for us no matter what someone else may tell you. There is victory in God's plans.

We may have planned in our life to marry someone, and things did not work out on your plans. It is imperative to understand it was not in the plans of God. It is essential to get clarification from God before making any decision in your life. God's plans are always better for us, and things will go in the right directions when the Lord leading the way in our life. The enemy will sometimes try to make bad things happen in your life, and it is not the will of God.

It imperative to understand that God is on our side, and the Lord will fight for us. God will turn things around in our favor in life. We just have to trust God, and never doubt the word of the Lord for our life. There is victory in God's plan. It does not matter what someone else think about your life. The plans God has for us is far beyond what anyone can ask or think. Have you ever wonder what God has for you?

Yes, what God has already plan for your life it belongs to you, and no one else can take it away from you. We can truly depend on the promises of God. The plans of God have for our life better than any man or woman promise us.

God's Blessing Plans

God has a set time when he desires things to take place in our life. The tests in life sometimes may get a little rough along the way. God plans is better the test, and your blessings is on the other side of your trails. We must remember in life quitting is not an option. God always has sometime greater for us, and it does not matter how we may feel about the situation.

God plan is better for our life, and trusting God is the right thing to do. Example, Daniel was throw into the lion den, and Daniel prayed three times a day. We have read the teaching of Daniel in the word of God, and he was placed in the lion den.

Daniel was a man of great faith, and trusted God to deliver him out of the den of lions. "Than this Daniel was preferred above the president, princes, because an excellent spirit was in him, the King thought to set him over the whole realm" (KJV).

God's Blessing Plans

There was a King name Darius, now the King of Babylon, and the other men was jealous of Daniel, and they tried to make Daniel lose his position. The men came together, and talk to King Darius to put Daniel in a den with some lions.

The men could not find no fault in Daniel to stop him from ruling in his position. "Hast not thy sign a decree, that everyman that shall ask to a petition of God or any man within thirty days, save of thee, O king shall be cast in the den of lions" (KJV). The men had a decree signed to try stop Daniel from praying unto God. It was a plan the men and King Darius put together, and they knew Daniel was going to be caught praying.

These jealous men had heard, and seen Daniel praying, and placed him the lion den to be eaten up. The next morning, they went back to see was Daniel eaten up by the lions. The enemy had a plan try to destroy Daniel in the lion den. It is imperative to understand Daniel life was in danger.

Daniel was not afraid of the plan the enemy trying to destroy his life. There was complete victory in God's plan, and God shut the mouth of the lions. Yes, no man has all the power over God's hands in this earth to out smart God's plans.

The men went back the next day to see if Daniel was alive in the lion den. The blessings of the Lord were all around Daniel in the lions' den. The lions fall asleep, and Daniel laid his head on the lion for a pillow. The enemy had a plan to try and destroy Daniel, and the enemy plan fail. There is always victory in God's plan.

One day, many years ago when I was young the enemy had a plan, and tried to destroy my life. The enemy stood in my face, and spoke evil words to me. My heart was pounding, and tears flowing down my face, and praying unto God for deliverance that day.

The enemy started backing up from me, and drop their head tears flowing down their face. The enemy had a plan to try do harm to me, and they could not do it. "Till I will make your enemy your foot stool" (KJV). God had his hands on me even as a young child even while in school.

I didn't fully understand everything at a young age. I can remember hearing some older people praying, God keep your hands on my children, and keep a hedge build up around them every day. There was a lot of things I could not understand as a child what older adults would say in their prayer time with God. I was happy God protected me from the enemy plans. The enemy left me alone, and never tried to come up against me again. The individual had become my best friend forever.

God's Blessing Plans

"The effectual prayers of righteous man availeth much"
(KJV). The prayers that was sent up for me even as a baby
God heard it. There is victory in God's plans every time,
and the devil can't stop God's plan.

We must continue to call on God, and he will come to
our rescue any week, day, and any time. It is a blessing that
God will come to us, when we call on his name Jesus. The
Lord is so awesome in all his ways, and there is nothing
God want, do for us. God is always sitting up high, and
looking down low on us every day of our life. I know for
myself God is a on time God, and never late.

"In my distress I called upon the Lord, and cried unto my
God; he heard my voice out of his temple, and my cry came
before him, and even into his ears" (KJV). David's was
being attacked by Saul, and other enemies trying to destroy
him on every side. God heard the cry of David, and rescue
him that very hour.

God's Blessing Plans

The enemy thought they had David in a corner, and he could not get out of a bad situation. "He delivered me from my strong enemy, and from them that hated me: for they hated me" (KJV). David had confidence in God no matter how much he went through with the enemy trying to destroy his life. There total victory in God's plan.

We are always in good hands with God no matter what kind of problems arise in our life. "When I cry unto thee, than shall mine enemies turn back: this I know; for God is with me" (KJV). David knew without a shadow of a doubt God was going to deliver him from his enemy. It is imperative to trust God every step of the way it does not matter how large or small the situations appear in your life.

There a distinction when you are crying out unto God it shows desperation and meditation in God. It is showing enthusiastic faith, and trust in God sincere love, and the power of King Jesus to work in our favor. We have traits that lays inside of us example, personal helplessness, humidity, cry for mercy, total surrender, God's ability & power, faith, desperation, and to call on God.

It is essential to understand that God is the ruler of the whole universe. "Weeping may endure for a night but joy will cometh in the morning" (KJV). The tears that flow on my pillow was just temporary, and God wipe all my tears away. There is always victory in God's plan.

Sometimes it may felt like you been in the wrestling ring with a giant, and it is no good match. Yes, you are sometimes faced with a big situation in your life, and you can't let it defeat whom we are in God. It may seem like your head is almost going down on the mate, and it is not over until God says it's over.

It is imperative for us to understand not to fight against God's plans for our life. Sometimes God may want to take us in another direction to receive our blessings. "The thief cometh not, but for to steal, and to kill, and to destroy: I am come that they might have life, and that they might have it more abundantly" (KJV) The enemy will try to falsely copy the plans of God.

The devil tries to make it look like it is God's plan. The Lord's plans are pure and genuine with no tricks in his plans. There is victory in God's plan everything fully guaranteed, and no gimmicks.

God's plans, there is a life time warranty that never goes out under no condition. The blessing of the Lord has power to keep us standing victorious in the battle in our life. Sometimes people may stand back, and look at us wonder how you going to come out on top in that situation in your life.

The plan we have chosen for life is the victory plan, and it is the greatest one on the earth today. Who plans are you following today? Let's do like Joshua "But for me and my house, we will serve the Lord" (KJV). There are so many different things people try to serve today, and they try to make a God out of it.

It is essential to understand God the true living, and is the best plan for our life today. What plan did God give Joshua to win victorious? We can easily define it in our text in three parts the Book of Joshua. God gave Joshua these plans to follow (1). A plan for the complete victory, 6:1-7, (KJV). (2). The total direct path to the victory, 6:8-2, (KJV). (3). The true promise to accomplish the full victory, 6:22-27, (KJV). The plan that God gave Joshua to follow was victorious.

"It came to pass, when the people heard the sound of the trumpet, and the people shouted with a great shout, and the walls fell down flat, so the people went up into the city, every man straight before him, and they took the city" (KJV). What walls are you facing in your life?

This wall could be your job, children, income, business or your health God can do what man thinks impossible. There is no wall big or wide enough for King Jesus. God has the power, authority to move out any obstacle from your path. Trusting God is in the plan to receive the total victory in our life.

God's Plan is to Communicate with us

It is imperative that God speaks to us and help every individual to make sound decisions in life. God first created Adam, and employed him to work in the garden to keep it clean, and grow food.

There was also Noah, and God communicated with him to build an Ark to help protect him, and his family from the flood that was coming upon the earth. Moses, was an awesome man that God spoke to in a burning bush, and told Moses take his shoes off on Holy ground he was standing on.

God's Blessing Plans

God is speaking to us today on different levels, and issues that surrounding us every day of our life. There is different ways God communicate with us, and it is essential for us to listen to the voice of God. How do you know when God is speaking to you? God will speak to you while reading his word, and a spoken word from his prophet or prophetess.

The preaching of the gospel, dreams, and visions, the word of God will breath life in us to help to you survive any task in your life. "All scriptures is given by inspiration of God, and is profitable for doctrine, for reproof, for correction" (KJV). God will speak to us letting us know when something is right, and God will make us see our wrong.

It is imperative we communicate with God through his word, and praying. God wants our worship, praying time with him, and continue to give him all the Glory & Praise. It is imperative to listen to the precious words of God whisper in our ears as we journey throughout the day. "My sheep hear my voice, and I know them, and they follow me" (KJV). It is essential to know the voice of God speaking to us, and the plans for our life.

The devil always has a plot, and God always has a plan. Sometimes God will use a friend, cousin, teacher, neighbor, and parent to send his message to us. It is essential to understand sometimes it may be a warning, a blessing, and maybe Prophetic instructions from a prophet concerning our life. It is important to listen, and obey the commands of God, and our lives shall be filled with great blessings.

The plans of God is to communicate with him, and understand the will of the father. "The wisdom that comes from heaven is first pure; then peaceable, gentle, and is easy to be intreated, and full of mercy and good fruits, without partiality, and without hypo-crispy" (KJV). God's love is filled with joy, and understanding to commune with us.

God's Blessing Plans

It is imperative to stay in tone with God, and listen to his voice, and for God's divine plans for our life. Even in life, if we don't have no communication with God. It is essential to get connected with God. The Lord will lead you to a joyful life filled with a purpose. It is God desire to see us bless, and fulfill our life with his plans.

"For the joy of the Lord is your strength" (KJV). When, we are communicating with God, and to bring clarification in our life to endure trouble times. The Lord is Mighty in powerful to bring peace during your situation, and to stop the wind from blowing in our life.

The greatest position to be in the whole world is in the arms of Jesus. It is imperative to understand man plan is nothing like God's directions for us. The ways of Lord are always right, and he will never go slack concerning his promise for our life.

Chapter -2

How to Stay in God's Plan

There are nature things in life we must follow in life for the laws of the land today. There are different laws we must follow to keep safe in the world. Example, we have traffic lights to obey, and it lets us know when to stop and go on a busy highway every day.

It is imperative to make these laws to keep everyone safe. There is so many things in life that may try to throw us off track with God. It is essential to stay in God's plan. "Enter ye in at the straight gate, and broad is the way that leaded to destructions, and many there be which in threat" (KJV). The enemy will try to tempt you in so many ways, and try to destroy you.

It is imperative to listen for God voice before making a move. The plan that God desire for us is so pure, righteous, and holy before the Lord. "Because straight is the gate, and narrow is the way, which leadeth unto life, and few there be to find it" (KJV). The plan of God must be carried out the right way.

It is imperative to do it God's way, and everything will work out in God's plans. There is victory in God's plans every time, and the right directions. Sometimes you may feel like you are all alone, and just remember God is right there with you all the time. The enemy will make you think everything alright on that crowd road, and nothing is going to happen to you.

Sometimes in life we may think taking a short cut is the right plan. It is essential to understand taking the quick way out sometimes may lead to destructions. Yes, sometimes trying to go at fast pace can lead you in a large crowd, and a lot of travels on that road.

God's Blessing Plans

Example, it is like getting caught up in heavy traffic on a rainy day, and everyone trying to reach their destination. A driver is   trying to exchange lanes, and all sudden someone had an accident. These are the these are the different things that happens in life, and it can be avoided if we just slow down and wait. It is imperative to follow God's plan, and don't try to make our own plans.

It is essential we don't get on the wrong road in life. God already have the plans for our life before we even born on the earth. "Let the redeemed of the Lord say so, whom he had redeemed from the hands of the enemy" (KJV). The plans of God for our life is to serve the Lord, all the days of our life.

The plans that God has for us to live, and to be used for his Glory. There is no other plan greater than King Jesus. God wants us to walk in his ways, and not on the road of the destruction. It is imperative we don't drift over in the wrong path. Sometimes an individual maybe wondering

their life away in a circle for many years.

God wants us to continue the right journey, and don't get

distracted by the tricks of the enemy. It is imperative to

seek the face of God every day for his guidance, and stay

on the right path in life. The right road in life have a lot of

benefits to live by every day.

It is essential to understand in God's plans there is

benefits you can count on. There is victory in God's plan,

and it is a guarantee while serving the Lord. It is important

to read the word of God, and this is the right plan for us to

stay healthy, and alive.

The importance of staying in God's plans.

It is imperative to stay with God's plans, and not mans. It

is God's desire to prosper us in every part of our life. We

have seen the plans unfold for Simon and Andrews in the

word of God. The word of God is filled with power and demonstration relating to his plans for our life.

The Lord know the directions we need to follow, and it is essential for us to trust God all the way. "For I know the thoughts that I think towards you, saith the Lord, thoughts of peace not of evil, to give you an expected end" (KJV). God knows what plans is right for our life, and Jesus is the best answer for us.

Example, we are sitting down trying to put a puzzle together and make a complete picture. We may pick a small piece of the puzzle and it does not fit in that spot. Sometimes our life feels like a puzzle, and we try to figure out the complete details.

God is the potter, and we are the clay shaping and model us for his desire purpose. It is not meant for us to know all the complete details in our life all at once. God already knows the plans even the day we were created. Life is always a continuing process every day, and it is imperative to stay in God's plan.

We may not be able to understand the full aspect at that minute, and it is imperative to just learn to be still, and let God. It is essential to stay in God's plan don't move to the left nor right. We must continue to trust God with all the blue prints he has for our life. The love God has for us greater than anyone could even think or believe on this earth. There is a blessing staying in the plans of God, and trusting the Lord with all your heart.

Yes, staying in God's plans, and we can earn all the blessings that stored up for you. The plans of God are so rewarding to fulfill our life with his love, knowledge, and help us to stay on the right path. The importance of keeping God's plan it will teach us how to love one another every day of our life, and live a Christian life.

God's Blessing Plans

It is essential to understand without being in God's plan we could not be happy, and you will not be able to love anyone in life the right way. God's plans will show us how to love everyone regardless if your enemy don't like you. "Be kind to one another, tenderhearted forgiving one another, as God in Christ forgave you" (KJV). This is a part of God's plan to show love to everyone, and never turn away from the Lord. It does not matter what we are facing God will take care of us.

Once we have realized the importance of staying in God's plan, and then it is easy to trust God. There gifts God's have blessed us with to be used for his Glory. It is imperative to allow God to manifest his blessings in our lives. The knowledge of God is so powerful, and it is so beautiful to behold in our hands. It is essential to stay in tuned with God in prayer.

God's Blessing Plans

God knows the right plans for you

It is important to listen to God, and not to people with the wrong directions for your life. Sometimes people try to go ahead of God, and do things there way. It is imperative to understand when we try to do things our way, and it may turn into a complete mess.

Sometimes individuals might feel like things will not work out for them the right way. It is essential to have faith in God, and let the Lord guide you the right directions in life. Sometime things may look a little impossible from the beginning on your journey.

It is the trick of the enemy trying to make you think things are not going to work in your favor. "Now faith is substance of things hope for, the evidence of things not seen" (KJV). Yes, we may not be able to see things with our nature eyes all the time, and it does not mean God stop working for you behind the scene.

God's Blessing Plans

We must always remember that our timing is not God's ways of doing things for us. God's plans are always the best plans for our life no matter how the enemy may try to play tricks in your mind. Sometimes it may be hard for you to believe God will bless you abundantly. Jesus loves us just that much to give his people the best in life. Sometimes the enemy wants to make you think less of yourself, and instead of believing the best for your future.

The plans that God has for us, and it will not always be reveal instantly in our life. It is imperative not to move before God, and mess things up in your life. Example, a flower is first become a seed in the ground than it began to grow with a stem, leaves, and blossom into a beautiful flower.

The blessings that God wants for us is more than you can imagine in your life. It is imperative never to doubt want God's plans for your life. "Looking unto Jesus the author and finisher of our faith" (KJV). We must continue to trust

God's Blessing Plans

God with all our heart, and not turn away from the blessing of God in your life. God's plans are the right choice for you today.

We can't predict our own future in life only God knows every plan for us. Sometime in life, men or women will promise to give you a gift, and it doesn't always turn out the way it was planned for you. The blessings that God promised will always remain in your life, just keep trusting, and following Jesus plan.

Sometimes things happen in our life, and we don't understand the reason for that storm landed in your life. It is imperative to understand that every problem that arise in your life, and it does not always affect everyone the same way. You may have asked this question, God why is this situation happening in my life? It is imperative to understand for every problem in your life God always has a solution. The plans of God is the right choice for you.

God's Blessing Plans

Our God has all seeing eyes, and knows our every cry. We may think our plan may be the right plan to overthrow your battle. God already knows our every need in life, and the correct plan for our life. There is no need for us to get upset with the things going on around us. "The name of the Lord is a strong tower: the righteous run into it, and is safe" (KJV). It is imperative to stay with God's plan that right for us, and when will never go wrong.

God's Plans is to Prosper You.

It is a part of God's plans to prosper us, and do the will of the Lord. It is essential to walk in the ways of God to receive the blessings in your life. "Beloved, I wished above all things that thou mayest prosper and be in health, even as thy soul prospereth" (KJV). God wants us to prosper, and live a heathy life, and do everything the right way.

God's Blessing Plans

It is important to have the right relationship with God,
and stay in God's plans. There is victory in God's plan, and
the miracles will be revealed in your life. God will take
good care of his people, and God will never leave you
alone.

Sometimes the enemy will try to make you think God not
for you. "The thief cometh not, but for to steal, and to kill,
and to destroy: I am come that they might have life, and
that they might have it more abundantly" (KJV). Walking
in the fullness of God is the best plan to keep in your life.
You want to have to worry about the enemy tricks and
games against you. Sometimes in our life things look a
little complicated, and you trying to figure sometimes out
in your life.

Example, a cross word puzzle you try to place all the
words in the right block, and solve it. Yes, it seems to be a
problem trying to find all the correct answer. We know
somewhere deep down inside there is a blessing waiting for

us. Sometimes you can feel the doors getting ready to open for you a blessing from God.

God already knows the plans he has for our life before we even ask or think. "For I know the thoughts I think towards you, saith thought of peace and not evil, to give you expected end" (KJV). God already knows the plans for our life even before were existed on the earth.

It is essential not try to have another agenda for our life, and make a mess along the way. God's plans are more enjoyable, and a relaxing moment in our life. Sometimes things in life will make no sense to us, and it is the right perception for God.

It is imperative to understand things does not go the way we want it all the time. It may not be the time frame that God desire to release your blessing in that season. "And we know that all things work together for good to them that love God, to them who are the called according to his purpose" (KJV). God has reasons for everything, and our destiny is in the Lord hands.

There are five things concerning God's promises for us. (1). The certainty of a promise. The verse clearly states, "we know that all things work together for good" (KJV). The scripture clarifies this is happening right now, and not suggesting a maybe for you. Sometimes it may look like God's plans is not working in your life. It is imperative we never try to go before God's plans for your future.

The next thing is (2) completeness in the promises of God, and it is already done. God is an awesome instructor, and desire to test us through different circumstances in life. We will learn a lesson for making our mistakes, and even through hardship in life. Sometimes your life may feel like it is on a roller coaster ride, and you don't know what to do. God is already got a plan to bring you out of the storm in your life.

God's Blessing Plans

Example, there may be some things you had experience on the job, and even in your home. The enemy is always trying to sit a trap, and God has the right plans in his hands to get you out of the valley.

It does not matter how hard the enemy tries to pull you back, and God's plans will deliver victory in your life. "I will never leave thee, nor forsake thee" (KJV). You, will sometimes get a little afraid when someone promise to wait for us, and they walk off leave you standing in a strange place alone. God always have the right plans for our life. It does not matter what it may look like in your life right now God knows best for you. God is awesome in all his marvelous works he created us with his powerful hands.

There is nothing never too hard about God's plans, and the creator of the whole universal will never let you down. It is imperative we should never try opining out God's plans for our life. We should be still and trust God all the way for our blessings. Sometimes it may look like those plans are slow developing the outcome. It may appear to you like a jag saw puzzle, and you can't put it together. "And we know that all things work together for good to them that love God, to them who are called according to his purpose" (KJV). God is still working everything out just for you, and it is already in God's plan.

It is essential to stand still and watch God prosper your hands for the good. It is God's desire to bless you. "Let the God joy and be glad, that favor may righteous cause: yea let them say continually, let the lord be magnified, which hath pleasure in prosperity of his servant" (KJV). God is always concern about us, and God desires to take care of our necessity in our life. It is imperative to understand that God came to give us more abundantly in our life, and we should never go in lack. It is in God's plans to prosper us.

God's Blessing Plans

God will not harm you

It is imperative to understand that God loves us every day of our life. The love that God has for you no man or woman can take his place. Sometimes the enemy will try to do things to harm you. God will never harm us for no reason in our life. God's love is so awesome, and it is a blessing to feel the Master's touch.

God's love is 100% guarantee, and there is no failure. I have experienced in my past life in a relationship, and fall in love with this young guy thinking that things would last for a life time. Yes, sometimes when you are young, and feel like this is the right person for you. Somewhere along the way the relationship began to go wrong, and things began to change in your life.

It is essential to understand sometimes things changes, and we must go on in life. The heartaches the enemy try to bring in your life, and may try to harm you physically or mentally. "The thief cometh not, but for to steal, and to kill, and to destroy" (KJV). The enemy plan is to keep you bound, and unhappy. God's plan is to keep us happy and free in our everyday life. It is not God's plan to harm us in any way. "I come that they might have life, and that they might have it more abundantly" (KJV). God has come to establish our hearts, and minds to be free. It is imperative to understand that God loves us so good that he allow his son Jesus to die on the cross for us.

Jesus hung on the cross for our sins, sickness, pain, and disappointments in life. "Beloved, I wish above all things that thou mayest prosper and be in health, and even as thy soul prospereth" (KJV). The love that God have for us today more than we can image. There is no disappointment in God's love for our life. God will keep us in his arms, and comfort us during our struggles in life. It is a blessing to know God will not leave you along the way. The natural things in life does not always last or was not meant to be for you.

God always have a better plan for our life. Sometimes we may feel like life is not fair at that moment. It is imperative to wait on God's plan for our life, and never try to figure out things in our behalf in live. There is no one else could every love us like God. "For God so love the world, that he gave his only begotten son that whosoever believeth in him shouldn't perish, but have everlasting life" (KJV). It is the love of God, and he cares enough for us to sacrifice his only son Jesus for us. It is nothing but love that God shown us, and the Lord will never cause us any harm.

What is harm? The word harm means to cripple, afflict, injury or hurt someone. Jesus didn't come to harm us only to love, and save us from sins. Sometimes people may tell you they love you, and their heart is far from it. The real true love of Jesus will bring you joy, peace, and happiness in our life.

God's Blessing Plans

There are different types of love that may be shared in our life. The storge love is found in the word of God it relates to Martha and Mary, and they lost their brother Lazarus. It is imperative to have this same type of love in our homes today. Abraham had a strong love for his son, and Noah also had a storge love for his wife and family. It is in God's plan to show love, and not to bring harm among our friends, and love ones.

Yes, this is same type of love our husbands and wives should desire for one another in a marriage. Storge love is a Greek word means (στοργή) for family love and frequently used for natural affection. We should have natural feelings to care about our love ones in life. The word love shows actions, and we say I love you it is expressing our feelings for someone. It is all in God's plans to show love, and the Lord will never bring us harm.

God's Blessing Plans

God's Has Plans for Your Future

The plans we have in mind may not be what God desire for us. It is imperative to listen to God's plans for your life. When should never move to fast in a matter, and it can cause total interruption to happen in our life. It is imperative to listen to God's voice, and go at the right time to receive your blessing.

There is nothing too hard for God to do for you, and your family. "But my God shall supply all your need according to his riches on glory by Christ Jesus" (KJV). Therefore, God already knows what we have need of before asking in prayer. I am so grateful God is not like woman or man. Example, we may ask our friend to do something for you, and they don't have time.

David was a mighty man of God, and desired to follow the plans of the Lord. "Now therefore so shalt thy say unto my servant David, Thus saith the Lord, I took thee from the sheepcote, from the following sheep, to be ruler over my people, over Israel" (KJV).

Now God had to send Nathan to tell him the plan was to build a house, and stay in it. It was already in God's plan for David life to someday become King. It is essential understand God already had our destiny, and even before we were in the world. God made David a King over Israel and Judah, and it is imperative to do God's will in our life. When we are disobedient it may cost us, and miss the plan God has for us.

We are God's children, and he loves us enough to give his people great gifts. "But ye are chosen generation a royal priesthood, an holy nation, a peculiar people; that ye shew the praise of him who had called you out of darkness into the marvelous light" (KJV). Yes, God has placed his approvable on our life, and to walk in the blessing plan.

God's Blessing Plans

"In that I command thee this day to love the Lord thy
God, to walk in his ways, and to keep his commandments
and his statutes and his judgments, that thou mayest live
and multiply: and the Lord thy God shall bless thee in the
land whither thou goest to possess it" (KJV). It is
imperative we continue to stay in God's blessing plan to
receive what the Lord has for us.

Sometimes the enemy will try make you think there no
good future for you. It may look like nothing is going right
in your season in life. It is just like planting vegetables in
our garden there a certain season it must be planted, and it
will grow. God has a season for us to excel in life, and it is
on the Lord's time table.

"For my thoughts are not your thoughts, neither your
ways, saith the Lord" (KJV). It does not matter how we feel
the plan should go for our life. God already has our plans in

his hands, and we were already predestinated in our mother's womb.

"Thou knowest my down sitting and mine up raising, thou understanding my thoughts afar off" (KJV). It is a blessing that God already knows us inside, and out. It does not matter what position we are sitting, and laying down, standing up God knows exactly what we are thinking all the time.

There is no one like God, and we can nerve measure up to the Master. "O taste and see that the Lord is good: blessed is the man that trusted in him" (KJV). It is imperative to put all our trust in God. When we, totally trust God, and God's plans will not fail you in life.

It is essential to stop and take time, and listen to God speaking to us. The hands of God are filled with wonderful blessings for us. There is nothing greater than the love of

God's Blessing Plans

Jesus in our home. Sometimes the enemy will try make us think that God's plan is not faster, and better.

Have you ever thought about a happy future? Yes, we all have dreamed, and desire the best in life. It is imperative as citizens living in the United States to get a good education, work hard, and have a beautiful life.

We have dreams to prosper, and live a comfortable life. God wants us to first serve him, and have the things in our life. It is essential not to let nice gifts to overtake us, and forget about God. We must not never misunderstand the plans of God for our life.

Sometimes along the way things may look a little dim, and you try to understand God's plans. It is essential to realize the Lord does not always show us everything on the same day. There are some things we must go through, and be prepared to reach the right place in God. Example, it is like you taking a test in class, and you don't know the question that is going to be on the test, until we get your test paper.

It is essential to understand we do not always know every complete detail God is working out for us. It is a process, and the plans are in the Masters hands. It is essential we should never get discourage when things don't seem to come quick, fast, and a hurry for you.

"But they that wait upon the Lord shall renew their strength; they shall mount up with wings as eagles, they shall run, and not be weary; they shall walk, and not faint" (KJV). You, must wait until God's plans to manifest in your life. Sometimes we find ourselves trying to figure everything out. It is not in our time frame. "And we know that all things work together for good to them, that love God, to them who are called according to his purpose" {KJV). Yes, it is imperative we stand still, and let the Lord have his way in our life.

God's Blessing Plans

Sometimes, we try to stick our hands in the matter and make our own plans, and create a big mess. It is imperative to stand back, and try to avoid making any mistakes in our life. The mercy of God, and it is so wonderful the Lord come to see about us. God is good to us all the time, and cares enough about our future. We should transform our mind to a new way of thinking about our future. We must be changed by the word of God. "For I know the thoughts that I think toward you, saith the Lord, thoughts of peace, and not of evil, to give you expected end" (KJV). It is essential to understand that God already knew us before we were ever produce on the earth by the Masters hands.

It is essential we don't walk in the wrong direction, and trying to predict our own future. It is important to allow God to lead us in the right path for our future in life. The plans of God are more rewarding, and satisfying that no man or woman eyes can ever behold the future.

Chapter 3

God's Plans Will Give You Peace

Sometimes the enemy will try to bring many distractions in our life. God will give us peace during any situation in our life. There is no greater love than Jesus Christ. There are some things we may go through in our home, and don't understand the reason for the problem.

Have you ever felt like your situation was worrying you? The God we serve is big enough to solve every problem big or small. "Let not your heart be troubled; ye believe in God, believe also in me" (KJV). It is just the trick of the enemy that tries to bring the lack of encouragement in your home, job, school, and family.

God able to give us peace the midst of every circumstance in our life. "These things I have spoken unto you, that in me ye might have peace" (KJV). God is saying I promise you peace no matter what the problem may look like in your life. Example, we may feel like being on a merry- go around, and you wonder when it is the trouble going stop interfering with your mind.

I can recall a personal matter in my life, and it seem like things was not getting no better for me. One day, I heard the voice of God speak to me in the midnight hour. "Thou will keep him in perfect peace, whose mind is stayed on thee: because he trusted in thee" (KJV). God was letting me know to trust him in everything that is going on in my life.

Sometimes the enemy will try to make things look bigger than it really appears. God had given me peace in the midnight hour. "In this world ye shall have tribulation: but be of good cheer; I have overcome the world" (KJV). Our Lord, Savior, Jesus, Christ have already died on the cross just for us, and to give us peace, love, and healing. God is a

God of that peace that unspeakable, and we can always feel the Lord's in our life. We never should guess the peace of God in our life. Oh, when God shows up we can feel his present all over us inside, and out.

The devil always has a plot but God has a plan for our life. The plans of God are so much better than man can do in a life time. Sometimes it may feel like we are trapped in a corner and there is no way out. God is the way out of the storms and struggles that may come your way.

How do we get out of a situation that seems impossible to woman or man but not impossible for God to fix in our life? It is imperative for us to trust God in every area in our life. We first must have a relationship with God, pray, fast, and study the word of God. "The effectual fervent prayer of a righteous man availeth much" (KJV). When we pray it will bring about a change in our life, and it does not matter how large or small it may seem.

God's Blessing Plans

Why it does not matter how big or little it is in our life, the problem may appear? There is nothing too hard for God to handle for us. Sometimes things may look crazy, and feel odd in your life. God has the right answer for us every time, and he will never leave you without a response. It is essential to stay connected to God, and never give up during your struggles.

When we pray it will bring about peace in the darkest hour of your life. "And the peace of God which, passeth all understanding, shall keep your hearts and minds in prefect peace" (KJV). The peace of God will allow us to think right, and help us make the right decisions.

God always has a winning plan for our life, and you can never lose. The devil has a plot, and God always a plan for our life, and it is filled with peace. "The thief not but for to steal, and to kill and to destroy: I am come that they might have life, and they might have it more abundantly" (KJV).

God's Blessing Plans

In this life, that we live God able to give us peace. The enemy will try to steal our dreams, peace, hope, and the love we have for one another.

It is essential to stay in God's plans, and trust the Master all the way. "Thou will keep him in perfect peace, whose mind is stayed on thee because he trusted in" (KJV). The plans of God will give you perfect peace. When we have the peace of God on the inside of us, and it will reflect in our home, job, community, in the church.

The peace of God is a joy to experience in our life. There is nothing like relaxing, and joying life every day. The power of God will keep us free from stress, and confusion in our life. It imperative to understand when we have peace, and the right relationship with God it make life much easier to live.

God's Blessing Plans

God's Plans Will Keep You

It is imperative to understand God's plan will keep us.
We can't keep ourselves in this world we live in today.
How can God's plan keep us? The word of God is so rich,
and powerful able to keep us from any hurt harm or danger.

There is nothing too hard for our God if we want to be
kept in these trying times. The God we serve is big enough
to do what man thinks is impossible. God able to do
everything without us wondering about anything going on
in our life.

God has so much compassion in his heart, and desires to
help us. God's plan is the best plan. There is so many kinds
of plans we can incorporate in our life, and a few plans will
work. The plans that God has for us a life time guarantee.

Example, we can plan to take a trip and things may not
work out right, and we may have to change the date. Our

God's Blessing Plans

God has a plan for us, and that plan will never change on us. "I come that they may have life, and that they may have it more abundantly" (KJV). God wants us to live a life filled with happiness, and in the right relationship with God.

The enemy will try to come and rob your future. "The thief cometh not but, for to steal, and kill, and to destroy" (KJV). It is essential to understand the enemy come to play for keeps with your life. The devil those not have nothing to offer you but pain, and a miserable lifestyle. Example, the enemy will make you think there is peace in partying, and hanging out. No, this is not a good life to live, and causes heartaches, pain, confusions, and staying broke with your money.

It is imperative to choose God's plan, and live a better life. The plan of God will offer you the rich abundance of living a healthy life spiritually, and nature. How does

God's Blessing Plans

God's plan give me an abundant life? The plan of God has

for us not just only gives us material things, and it also

allows us to have a peace of mind.

It is essential to look at this in spiritual realm, and in the

nature. "Therefore if any man be in Christ, he is a new

creature: old things are passed away; behold all things are

become new" (KJV). We are now walking into a new plan

for our lives. We no longer think, act, look, and do the

same things as in the past. We are now living a new life,

and everything has changed about us inside and out.

The blessings of God are upon our life now, and we are

living in the abundances. The abundant life is more than

material things on this earth. The word of God is true

throughout the world which we live in today.

"Now unto him that is able to ask exceeding abundantly

above all that we ask or think, according to the power that

worketh in us" (KJV). God able to bless us to live an

abundant life, and it is according to our faith in God to receive our blessings. God loves us enough that he wants us to get the right plan for our life.

What does abundance mean? It is to have a plenty more than enough overflowing, large quantity, ample, sufficient, and adequate. God's plan is just that good to allow these blessing to come in our life. It is imperative to choose God's plan for your life.

There may be some situation in your life, and God is right there all the time. "But my God shall supply all of your needs according to his riches and glory by Christ Jesus" (KJV). God able to take care of your needs, and keep us in his plans. God's plan is the best life to live.

I can remember hearing the older people use to say God got it all in control. I didn't understand what they were saying at that time. We know God is all powerful, and a knowing Master of the earth. As, I look back over my life now, and it is clear to me in the word of God.

The older generation was saying God able to take care of them, and the family. There was a lot of things the older people went through many years ago. It is essential to understand the older saints of God trusted the Lord. They prayed and sing unto the Lord, and they never doubted the promises of God. It didn't matter how the problem was looking to them from the inside or outside. The plan of God was greater than their circumstances.

It is imperative for us to keep our faith in God, and never doubt. "Now faith is the substance of things hope for, the evidences of things not seen" (KJV). Yes, the elderly always prayed unto God, and kept the faith that God is coming to their rescue. We have learned a lot from the older people, and our love ones.

God's Blessing Plans

There are some of us taught through hearing the word of God in church every Sunday morning. Once, we keep hearing the word preached it began to take effect in our heart. It is imperative to understand after hearing the word we must put it into action. "But be ye doers of the word, and not hears only, deceiving your own self" (KJV). We must exercise our faith, and believe God will take care of us. Example, we believe the car will crank, and if you didn't connect the battery post to the battery it will not crank up.

We need a positive connection with God, and believe the abundance of blessings will come in our life. "But without faith it is impossible to please him: for he that cometh to God must believe he is, and that he is a rewarder of them that diligently seek him" (KJV). God wants us to depend on him with all our heart, and mind. God's plans is the best one for us.

God's Blessing Plans

We can receive more abundance from God when receiving Jesus Christ as our Savior. It is essential for Jesus to be a part of our life, and we are enjoying the good news of Jesus Christ. God has the best plans for our lives.

Serving God is the right plan

Sometimes in life we think our plans will work well for us. Yes, somewhere down the road in life God interrupts our plans. "For my thoughts, neither are your ways my ways saith the Lord" (KJV). There are some things you tried to make it work in your life.

Is it the plans God desires for us? No, it is imperative to understand we was already predestinated in the hands of God. Only God knew about our birth, time, place, and our parents. Even before we had the mind to think for ourselves, and God already had our destiny written out for us.

God's Blessing Plans

"For as the heaven are higher than the earth, so are my ways higher than your ways, and my thoughts than your thoughts" (KJV). What we think is best for us not always the right plans. God know better than any of us, the Master does not make no mistakes.

Sometimes, we may think this is too big for us to handle. God already knew you was qualified for the position. It is essential to understand when God blesses us in a position, and there is already a seal placed on it from God. It is imperative to understand God's plan is always right for our life.

The world will try to offer you other bargains in life, and try to make you think this alright for you. The enemy is a counterfeit, and try to make somethings look like it is God. It is imperative to understand the tricks of the devil. The blessings of the Lord last forever for us. "The blessings of the Lord, it maketh rich, and he added no sorrow" (KJV).

God's Blessing Plans

When we are serving God there no need to worry about anything in our life. God will fill our lives with abundance of joy, peace, love, family, and money.

What are five ways we can serve, and follow God's plan for our life? Example, "And he said follow me, and I will make you fishers of men, and they straightway left their nets, and followed him" (KJV). Simon and Andrew life had now just begun in these two verses in God's word. God already had a plan for these two men of God. It is essential to understand that God plan is always right, and never wrong.

Yes, serving God is in the correct plan for us, and keeping the right relationship with God. We first have to trust God's judgment for our life. "For I know the thoughts that I think towards you, saith the Lord, thoughts of peace, and not of evil, to give you expected end" (KJV). The abundances of many blessing God has stored up for us. We must trust God, and continue serving the Lord every day of our life.

It is imperative to understand when we are serving God's plan to show love, and to help someone else in along the way in life. Whatever our mission is in life to serve the Lord. Our assignment maybe feeding the hungry, clothing, and sheltering the homeless. It is a blessing to serve and help others in a needy time in life. We must continue as true believers in Christ to follow the Master plans.

God has blessed everyone with a talent, and it is imperative to ask the Lord for directions for our life. "Them hath he filled with wisdom of heart, to work all manner of work of the engraver, and of the cunning workman, and of the embroider, in blue, and in purple, in scarlet, and in fine linen, and of the weaver, and even of them that do any work and of those that devise cunning work" (KJV). Moses was speaking to Israel about their skillful talent. God had blessed them with different gifts to use, and it was in the Masters plan for their life. Serving God and following the plans the Lord is the best plan.

It is important to stay connected to God in pray to find out the plans that Lord has for you. If you have any doubt about God's plans just seek the Lord in prayer. "And this is the confidence we have in him, that, if we ask anything according to his will he hearth us: And if we know that he hear us, whatever we ask, we know we have the petitions, we desired of him" (KJV). We truly are serving God, and in prayer you have the right to ask the Lord the plans for your life.

It is imperative to pray let God's will be done in our life. The will of God determines our subsequent steps to be take in our life. God will continue to show us the right way, and when we should stay in the present of the Lord. "Pray without ceasing" (KJV). We must continue to pray, and never stop praying. God wants us to communicate with him every day.

The plan of God has another requirement for us, and that is to love. It is imperative that we always show love towards one another as God has spoken unto us. "We love him, because he first loved us" (KJV). When we have the love of God on the inside of us, and it will allow us to love one another.

The plan of God is the best plan for our life. There is no one greater than the love of Jesus Christ. When we walk in the plan of God it will teach us to walk, and talk right. "That he would grant you according to the richest of his glory, to be strengthened with might by his Spirit in the inner man" (KJV).

The Spirit of God will give us the inner love deep down on the inside to follow peace, and love with everyone in Jesus name. "That Christ may dwell in your heart by faith, that ye, being rooted and grounded in love" (KJV). It is imperative to have the love of Christ abiding on the inside of us. It is essential to understand that without God in our life we can't love one another right.

The love of God in our life is the right plan for us. "This is my commandment, That ye love one another, as I have loved you" (KJV). God is so loving and cares about us, and God wants us to care for another as well.

The real love of God cares about everything we do, and the Lord don't let us go without anything in our life. "If a man say, I love God, and hateth his brother, he is a lair: he for he that loveth not his brother whom he hath seen, how can he love God whom he hath not seen" (KJV). When, it is spoken from our lips we love God, and you have never seen the Lord.

The love we have for God through communication in prayer. We can feel the love from God that keep drawing us in his present to commune. We are walking and talking

vessels of God, and should have the real love of Christ

living on the inside of us every day. The love of God

should be so strong we can feel our brother or sister in

Christ standing in need.

Example, there may be someone you want to show them

love, and while they are going through their trail in life.

Sometimes a encouraging word or a helping hand will

brighten their day. God plans is even filled with love, and

to help strengthen one another in love.

God created Adam and Eve to have someone to love, and

raise a family. It was all in God's plans to create man and

woman to be fruitful, and multiply on the earth. It is God's

will for the husbands and wives to do according to God's

plans. It is imperative to show love to one another, and to

live together, and show love as husbands, and wives. We

must demonstrate love to our children, families, and other

individuals that cross our paths in life. God's plan is the greatest one for us.

Chapter – 4

Trust God's Plan

We have heard the word trust. What does trust really means to you? Trust it means to have confidence in someone or something. There is truly one thing we may do, and that is to depend on God. It is imperative to understand the reliance on God will never fail us.

In times like these we need someone in our life to trust. There are things you may tell Jesus, and the Master want tell nobody else. It is a blessing to trust God with all our personal business in life. "Trust in the Lord with all thy heart; and lean not unto thine own understanding" (KJV). When we, put all our trust in God it is a guarantee relationship with God. It does not matter what time of day or night we can call on the Lord. God will always answer our cry even in the midnight hours.

Sometimes we may go through things, and you don't know how to handle the problem. I know there was a time in my life, and I were faced with a situation only God could solve for me. One night, I was tossing and turning in my sleep trying find the solution to my problem.

The answer came to me late in the midnight hour. "Come unto me, all ye that labour and are heavy laden, and I will give you rest" (KJV). God was speaking to me, trust him with my problems, and let him take care of it. I used to hear the older people use to say you can depend on God.

During that time, I was not understanding those words. I had to encounter sometimes in my life to get an invitation to try God for myself. Yes, it is essential to trust God for yourself. When, we develop the right relationship with God, and you can talk to King Jesus about anything in your life.

Yes, God wants us to communicate with him every day. It is something about calling on the name Jesus, and even the enemy will tremble cause their power in the name of Jesus. We, can call on the name Jesus, and the Lord will come to your rescue. The name Jesus will connect to your faith, and victory is in the name of Jesus. The plans of God are the right one for us.

"He that dwelleth in the secret place of the most High shall abide under the shadow of the all mighty" (KJV). When, we trust God, and the Lord will continue to take care of us no matter what the situations is in your life.

It is imperative to realize when rough times may appear in your life, and we can go to the rock which is Jesus

Christ. I found out in the early stages of my life, God will provide when we trust the Lord. God is not like man or woman telling you they got your back, and you look around they are nowhere in your present.

I used to hear this old lady say God is a rock in the wilderness. I didn't catch what this old woman was saying when I was a young girl. I asked the question one day how can Jesus be a rock? The old lady just looked and smiled at me, and said baby you may not understand it right now. The old lady told me one day you will understand it better by and by.

I will never forget what the little old lady told me. As I had begun to grow up, and found out about life it was imperative for me to talk to God about my problems. There were times in my life, I needed someone to lean on. God had brought everything back to my memories what the woman told me. I reached back at that testimony the old lady shared with me.

Jesus is my rock, and I can totally depend on God. When we, look around us today so many things man try to put their trust in the world. "Let not your heart be troubled: ye believe in God, believe ye also in me" (KJV). God will want us to trust him in everything we do in life big or small.

It is essential for us not to stay up, and worry about your problems. God is bigger than any mountain or river in our life. It is not the will of God for us to worry about the things of the world. Trusting God, and communicating with God is one of the key foundations to stay in tune with God. "Casting all your cares upon him for he caerth for you" (KJV). It is imperative we give all our burdens unto the Lord, and leave our problems in his hands.

God's Blessing Plans

God does not want us to live a stressful life, and living
unhappy. It is a blessing to trust God, and let the Master
take care of our situations in life. "Being careful for
nothing, but in every thing by prayer and supplication with
thanksgiving let your request be made know unto God"
(KJV). Trusting God is the most important step to take in
our life, and never doubt the Lord. Sometimes in life things
will look like it may be impossible, and we try to think
things out in our minds.

The enemy will try to put doubt in your heart. "for God
hath not give us the Spirit of fear; but of power, and of
love, and of a sound mind" (KJV). The love God has given
us the desire to put all our trust in him, and never fear about
anything going on around us. God able to keep us from all
hurt harm or danger that tries to come near our life.

There is no need of being afraid. "For in the time of
trouble he shall hide me in his pavilion: in the secret place

of his tabernacle shall he hide me; he shall set up upon a rock" (KJV). Sometimes it may look like things are falling apart around you. It is imperative to put all your trust in God. Trusting God is in the plans for our life, and the all Mighty King Jesus got it all in control. God's plans are the right one for us.

Keep your focus on God's plans

It is imperative to keep our focus on God's plans for your life. What is focus? Focus means to pay attentions to something going on. God wants us to stay focus in the plans he has for our life. It is imperative to understand keeping our eye on the Master plans. "Thou wilt keep him in perfect peace, whose mind is stayed on thee: because he trusted in thee" (KJV). Yes, our mind must be focus on God, and let him direct our path.

It is imperative to understand that if your mind is not focus on the plans of God, it is easy to miss your blessing.

God's Blessing Plans

When, your mind is side tracked, and it is hard to start back over to the beginning of the process. Have you, ever started doing something with a project, and you lost focus? Yes, we all have lost focus at least one time in our life, and you had to started over again on your project.

Example, planning a vacation for your family, and you had to focus on the place, season, and the best time to take your trip. It is essential to take your time, and make all the necessary plans including the cost of your vacation. It is imperative to stay focus and incorporate all the complete details before booking the trip.

When, we leave out something in the plans for our vacation. It will cause confusing with the trip not to be completely planned probably, and a disappointing vacation. We must be purpose driven with the plans God has placed before us to follow in life. It is imperative to understand not to let nothing or no one distract our focus in

God's Blessing Plans

God's plans for our life. God wants us to be happy, and live a peaceful life in the Lord.

"Calling a ravenous bird from the east, and the man executed my counsel from a far country: yea, I have spoken it, I will also bring it to pass; I have purposed it, I will also do it" (KJV). The plan that God has placed before us will come to pass. It is essential to stay focus in God's plans.

The plans that God has for our life, and it was already placed om motion for you. These plans are draw out by the Masters hands with complete details, and preparations, God already knew our DNA, and the complete assignment for life. God has the best plans for our life.

It is imperative to wait, and God will let you see your blue print for your life in details. Example, you may be planning go to baseball game than it began to rain, thundering, and lightening hits a light pole. The game was not cancelled because of the rain that day. The weather forecast said only 10% chance of rain.

The coaches cancelled the game for other reasons not cause of the rain. It was a blessing God allowed the game to be cancelled, and no one got hurt that day. It is imperative to listen to God plans placed before us. The plans of God are greater than any man made on the earth.

We may plan something else to do in our life, and God will turn our plan around to protect us from hurt, harm or danger. Yes, it is important to focus on the voice of God, and do things according to God's will for our life.

"The counsel of the Lord stands for ever the thoughts of his heart to all generation" (KJV). Sometimes we may have our own plans, and it does not work because it was not in God's plans. Example, sometimes a wedding planner may make a mistake, and leave out a simple detail in the wedding rehearsal.

God's Blessing Plans

When these types of things happen, it is a human error in
the eyes of man or woman. It is imperative to understand
that God is the best planner for our life. How you stop the
spirit of distract from entering your mind while walking on
your journey with God? It is essential not to allow certain
things to come in our life, and cause distraction to take
place. "Thou will keep him in perfect peace, whose mind is
stayed on thee: because he trusteth in thee" (KJV). It is
imperative keep our hearts and minds in prayer, and
reading the word of God to stay focus.

Everything we encounter in our is not always bad. It is
imperative we stay focus on God, and don't let things
distract us. There are some simple things we must deal with
in our life. Example, car, job, these are things sometimes
the enemy tries to use small issues, and try make it a large
problem.

The enemy will try to use these things as a distraction tool to try take our focus off God. We must stay focus on God through praying, fasting, and studying God's word. We should renew our minds every in Christ, and stay in tune with the Lord. God, wants to bless us, and King Jesus gets all the praise, and the Glory. The plans of God are the best for us.

Praise & Worship in God's Plan

It is imperative to worship God always, and never allow the enemy to control your life. The praises of God will keep your strength up while going through any test in your life. The Lord desires, is to help us in the time of our troubles. Sometimes people do not understand that God is always on your side through the thick and the thin. "And at midnight Paul and Silas prayed, and sang praises unto God: and the prisoners heard them" (KJV). The trap the enemy had sat for Paul, and Salas to be throw into prison only increase their faith to trust God for deliverance.

God's Blessing Plans

The enemy had a plot against these men just because they were God's chosen vessels to spread the Gospel of Jesus Christ. They were beaten, and throw into prison for loving God. The enemy had a plot, and but God had a plan for Paul, Salas life.

The place looked so dark, and they felt worry just for a little while in the prison. "And suddenly there was a great earthquake, so the foundations of the prison was shaken: and immediately all the doors were opened, and every one's bands were loosed" (KJV). The praises of God will stop the plot of the devil, and to drop their weapons cause the battle was already won in Jesus name.

The enemy did not like how God used Paul, and Salas to bring salvation, healing in that city. The plans of God's is always better than the plot of the enemy. It is imperative to get in the present of God giving him all the Glory, and praises. We must do like these men of God lift our hearts, and minds unto the Lord without fear.

God's Blessing Plans

It is essential to tone in the right channel with God, and allow the Lord to stop the plot of the devil. It is imperative to flow in the right spirit, and the peace of God will rest upon us. The power of God will take control in our life, and the plot of the enemy will be destroyed. "But thou art holy, O thou that inhabitest the praises of Israel" (KJV). God wants us to praise and worship in his present, and let him handle every situation in our life.

The plans of God is awesome, and it will out weights the devil plot every time. We should always "enter into his gates with thanksgiving, and into his courts with praise: be thankful unto him, and bless his name" (KJV). It is essential to honor the name of the Lord, and everything he has done for us. There are many wonderful things God has planned for our life.

Yes, it is imperative to keep a praise on our lips it will frightens the devil, and the enemy will fear when God shows up before him in the room. The enemy always think his plot can work, and God is victorious every time. "Whosoever offereth praise glorifieth me: and to him that ordereth his conversation aright will I shew the salvation of God" (KJV). God is desiring our praising unto him, and magnify his Holy name.

The praises of God will release his power to destroy the works of the devil. It is imperative for us to stay in the present of God through every situation in our life. The enemy will try to use all kinds of tricks to stop the plans God has for our life. The praises, and worshiping the Lord will help to overthrow the plot of the enemy. We have to release the praises of God in our heart, and it will allow God to fight the battles for us.

When, we praise God it is a powerful instrument to tear down the enemy territory. "No weapon that is form against you shall prosper" (KJV). There is power in our tongues to speak the word of God over our life. Example, the children of Judah was outnumbered by their enemy the army of

Ammon, Moab, and Seir. The people of God, and King Jehoshophat pray unto the Lord for an answer. God told them go ahead, and stand against the plot of the enemy, and he will fight the battle for them. "And when they began to sing and to praise the Lord set ambushments against the children of Ammon, Moab, and Mount Seir, which were come against Judah, and they were smitten" (KJV). There is power in praising God, and the devil will tremble when hearing the name Jesus.

The praises of God will cause the enemy to run from the plot he tried to set up against the people of God. There is no need to worry, and be afraid of the enemy plot because God already have your plans worked out. "Make a joyful noise until the Lord, all the earth; make a loud noise, and rejoice, and sing praises" (KJV). The plans of God are better for our life, and allowing the Lord to take control.

God's Plans Deserve the Highest Praise

The worship and praise unto the Lord is just like sweet music in God's ears. God cares about his people, and the Lord desires every praise from our lips. It is imperative to always lean on Jesus, and never give up no matter what the situation looks like in your life.

You may have got up this morning and your plans was to do five things on your list for today. During, the course of day, the time had passed by fast, and there were only two things completed on your list. It is essential to realize things do happen throughout the course of the day, and cause a shift in your plans. God has a way of changing things we desire to do. When things are happening in this order it simply means not the plans of God.

The enemy had a plot in the midst the plan. God able to turn things around for a reason in our life. There are different types of plans in our life, we may have to tried to enjoy. There were some exciting plans you already try, and enjoy a relaxing vacation with your spouse or family. Sometimes we may have planned this vacation for a year, and a week before the trip a love got sick. "Everything work together for the good for those that are called according to his purpose in Christ Jesus" (KJV).

I can remember the time we had plan to go back to Tennessee in the early winter part of the year, and we cancel the plans about two days before leaving for the trip. When, I cancel the trip to go to Tennessee, and the snow hit the same day we were supposed to leave on our trip.

God already knew the weather conditions before man had given any type of report concerning the snow. The snow in mountains that year had caused a lot wrecks to occur on the highways. It is imperative to listen to God, and follow his divine plans for our life. God always know the best things for us, and the Lord cares about our life.

God's Blessing Plans

Sometimes we may not understand the answer is no from God at that moment. There is always a reason in our life God allows for things to work out that way for us. I was thankful for obeying the spirit of God, and doing it the Lord's way. We were glad that God spoke to cancel the plans, and not to go that day. "Obey, God and not man" (KJV). It is the most important choice anyone can ever make in their life. Our lives are so precious today, and God loves us every day.

There may have been some serious consequences if we done things our way. "The devil come to kill steal and destroy" (KJV). The enemy could have tried to get in the midst the storm, and our lives may have been lost that day. "God came to give us life, and more abundantly" (KJV). There is so many blessing that God wants his people to receive in life.

God is the all-knowing God, and his eyes see all over the earth. There are things we never know without first seeking

God's Blessing Plans

God, and receive his plans for us. I rather have God's plans in my life than man. God's plans in my life will keep me happy and safe every day of my life. The enemy always has a plot to try destroy God's people. It is essential to understand God's plans will give us more benefits in life.

It does matter to God about our life, and it is imperative to stay before the lord. God has our plans the best blessing plans for us. Sometimes, we may look at a plan, and the enemy try to make us go ahead pick right now. I have learned from experience it not good to rush into making a quick decision in life. When, we rush and make a quick decision it is 75% chance you picked the wrong plan.

Life today is filled with making a lot choice, and being happy with your plan. Sometimes the enemy desire for us to make a mistake, and get into the wrong plan. The plan of God will release joy in our life.

"The joy of the Lord is our strength" (KJV). The joy God has given unto us the world didn't give it, and the world can't take it away. The plan of God is greater than any man on the whole earth. It is imperative to stay in God's plan, and not our own. "Walk in God's will not our own" (KJV).

Chapter 5

Blessings Plan of God in Our Marriage

It is God desire for us to be blessed with a spouse, and to live a happy life in God. The Lord wants us to first communicate with him every day and serve him for the rest of our life. It is imperative for us to have a mate which ordain by God even in the beginning of time.

God able to give us the love that we desire, by hands of the lord. "Let the husband render unto wife due benevolence and likewise also the wife unto thy husband" (KJV).

God's Blessing Plans

It is essential for us to follow the plans of God, and strive to do according the word of the Lord. The beauty of marriage is designed by the hands of God for husband, and wife to walk together hand in hand to be happy. The joy of a man is to be filled with the love of God, and to enjoy life on the earth.

The love of our Master, Jesus is so awesome in all his ways, and filled with so much compassion. The plans of God will always out weight the thoughts of man every time.

We can never out think God, and go before his plans that is design for our lives. Sometimes life seem to be a little confusing, and trying to find the right direction in your life. It is imperative to follow God the path that leads us to happiness.

The things the Lord desire for you is the right Master's plan. "The joy of the Lord is your strength" (KJV). God able to give you joy midst of a bad situation. The power of God is far beyond your imagination, and can't be touch with the stroke of a pen. The plan of God "love your wife as Christ loved the church" (KJV). Man, should love their wife like Christ loved the church, and there no limits, and nothing being held back in the relationship.

Jesus Christ, died for us, and there was no question asked about the situation. God still loves us unconditional, and even when we didn't know Jesus in the parting of our sins. God desire is for man to love his wife as Christ the church, and it is in God's plans.

It is imperative man first give their life to the Lord, and under the divine orders of Jesu Christ. The love of Jesus will flow into the heart of man, and walk in the obedience of God. Man's primary ministry that is in the plan of God to love your wife as a husband. It is the plans of God to first love the Lord that created us to live on the earth, and give Jesus all the praise. "Love your wife in the same way that you love your body and your life" (KJV). It is imperative that man stay well feed, clean, and healthy.

It is essential as a gentle man should look after his wife likewise, and make sure every need is meet. It is in God's plan for man to provide for his wife financially, emotional, and spiritual wellbeing to excel in life.

It is imperative that man love his wife, and take care her just as God planned in his word. "Call your wife blessed and praise her" (KJV). It is a blessing that God gave you a wife to share, and fulfill your dreams on the earth.

Women will desire to hear those special words coming from their husband lips to uplift her heart. God has made women to be special jewelry just for man to love, and take care of for the rest of their life. The true heart of a woman loves God, and the family to do according the Master's plans.

God's Blessing Plans

It is in God's plans for a man to compliment his wife, and loving the Lord. A good wife should be a wonderful mother, well manner, contributes to work. It is essential for man to show love, and appreciation for their wife. The devil has a plot, and God has a plan.

The plans of God are never short, and always will out power the enemy plots. God's eyes are open to see everything going on in our life. You may feel like it was the last ending in your relationship, and all the bases were loaded. It is imperative to keep your focus on God, and never get distracted.

You are standing still waiting for God to move according his plans for your life. Example, sometimes life feel like a baseball game you are at the plate, and a fast ball come your way. The first ball thrown is a curve, and it went by you. There is call batter up, and you are waiting to hit the ball. The ball came and almost knock you off the batter's mount.

God's Blessing Plans

The next ball came right even over the batter plate, and you knocked the ball out of the park. It is just like the enemy try to plot against you, and but God has a plan to keep us in his hands. It is imperative for you to stand still and let God show us the direction to take in life. Sometimes it will feel like the wind blowing so hard in your life, and everything is pressing against you. You can't give up, and that is the trick of the enemy for you to take down.

The things the devil will try to trap you into a life of hopelessness, and the enemy wants you to think no one loves you. The plans the God has for your life are greater than your nature eyes can see every day. It is the will of God you live a healthy life filled with love, and enjoying the blessings of the Lord.

It is imperative for husbands and wives to stay on one according, and stand in the word of God. It is essential for us to worship the Lord, and keep our children in the present of God to show forth love.

God's Blessing Plans

"Thou wilt show me the path of life: in thy present is the fullness of joy; at thy right hand, there are pleasures for evermore" (KJV). God already knows the path we must take in life, and the devil will try to throw a road block up try to stop you from getting to your destination. It is essential for us to understand that God wants to bless you, and your family.

The blessing of the Lord will come to bring you peace, and stability in your life. When the blessing of the Lord is in favor in your marriage, and good things happens in your life. Marriages are ordained by God, and it is even in God's plan to stand together in the trouble times.

Sometimes it may be a simple problem in your life that the enemy tries to bring distraction in your marriage. It was already in God's plans for man to be married with a wife, and live a happy life.

God's Blessing Plans

"Submitting yourselves one to another in the fear of God" (KJV). It is essential to continue to respect, and love one another always so the blessings of the Lord will remind in our house. It is imperative to stay in the present of the Lord even when you there are problems arrives in your life.

Sometimes there are things we may not understand the reason at that moment. It may seem like you are at all odds with the situation that the enemy tries attack you in life. "And we know that all things work together for good to them that love God, to them who are called according to his purpose" (KJV). Sometimes you may feel like there is no more hope, and the enemy trying to destroy your relationship.

God, already have a plan to fix that broken spot in your marriage. The hands of God able to put your marriage back on the wheel, and repair the broken places. The power of God can over take the plot of the enemy, and destroy the enemy in the time of trouble. "For in the time of trouble he shall hide me in his pavilion: in the secret of his tabernacle shall he hide me; he shall me up upon a rock" (KJV). During the disappointing times in your marriage God able to keep your relationship on course, and will not allow it to sink.

It is imperative to trust God even when things not looking good in your life. We must first put our trust in God, and never doubt. It essential to put God in your life, and allow the Lord to take control. We should cry out to God, and allow the Lord to take over your heart, thoughts, and our lips to give him praise.

It does not matter how small or big the devil plot is now, and our God always has a plan to deliver you. "Evening, and morning, and at noon, will I pray and cry aloud, and he shall here my voice" (KJV). God ears are always open to hear your cry it does not matter the time of day. God will stay near to help rescue you in the middle of a bad situation in your life.

God's Blessing Plans

It is in God's plans for our marriage to be fill with wonderful blessing in our house. Even in the middle of the plot the enemy throw out against you, and God able to use it to shape you into his purpose for your life. The blessings of the Lord are sweeter than you can ever image.

"I am with you always even unto the end of the world" (KJV). God is there for you when everyone else has walked away from you. There are so many things in life we can walk away from in life example, job, friends, and problems.

God will stick with you closer than a brother or sister. It is imperative to stand together in your marriage. When the challenges in life will try to push you off course, and turn against your mate. You should rest in God, and pray unto the Lord to give you the right directions.

The enemy will try to plot, and to distract you from the will of God for your life. The devil doesn't like to see nobody happy, and he tries to keep everything in a up roar all the time. The enemy had a plot, and God has a plan for your life. God will pour out a blessing in your life, and make you stronger.

It does not matter about the storm you may have faced in your marriage, God is still in charge of your life. There are somethings you can't change only God can do it for you. It is imperative we learn to trust in the Lord, and it may look like things are not going to work in your favor.

It is imperative to stay focus during hard times, and don't give up on your marriage. You are to bless, and do not even think about being stress. Jesus will see you through the rough time in your life, and quitting is not an option for you. "What therefore God but together, let no man put asunder" (KJV). It is God desire to see your marriage blessed, and not shifted into the outer courts of defeat. It is essential to walk in unity, pray, and keep the faith.

God's Plan Will Bless Your Home

It is the desire of the Lord to bless you and your family every day of your life. The relationship we must have with God it is important to follow the plans that sit before you to fulfill a success life. The enemy does not want to see you bless, and live happy with your family.

"The thief cometh nit, but for to steal, and to kill, and to destroy: I am cometh they might have life, and they may have it more abundantly" (KJV). It is imperative to keep your focus on God, and never get distracted.

Sometimes you, may have problems to arise in the home, and the enemy tries to come in keep us frustrated. Example, sometimes we may desire to build our a house one way. God desire is to build your house another style for you to live in even today. It is imperative to listen to God, and follow his plans for your life.

God's Blessing Plans

The plans of God are much greater than your thoughts every time. Our ideas can never outreach God's plans for our life. "For my thoughts are not your thoughts, and your ways are not my ways" (KJV). I learned in life things does not always go the way we plan it to work for us. It is imperative not to question God's plans for your life.

It is essential to allow God to bless your home, and allow the Lord to step in your life let him build your house. Example, building a house you must first lay a foundation, and working it up from the bottom. Yes, everything in life always have a starting point. It will always take time to get everything in order needed for your project.

It is imperative to understand just like a nature carpenter building a house you must follow the blue print through every step to complete the project. The house that God has for you, and it is special designed for you. There are different types of plans God has for us, and no two individuals have the same lay out. What plans do you have for your home today? Are you placing it all in God's hands to bless your home? The blessings of the Lord resting in your home will bring peace, and happiness. The devil had a plot, God has a plan to bless you.

"And I give unto them eternal life; and they shall never perish, and neither shall any man pluck them out if my hands" (KJV). It is imperative to rest in Jesus, and let God work in the present of your home, and family to live a peaceful life. God is the most important foundation to building our home, and living to accomplish the plans. The devil had a plot, God has a plan of victory for you

Sometimes the enemy will try to bring confusing in your home. It is imperative to allow the blessing of the God to rest in your house. God wants to bring peace during a bad situation right now in your life. "Neither be ye sorry for the joy of the Lord is your strengthen" (KJV). When we are walking in the love of Jesus it brings peace in our heart.

God's Blessing Plans

It is imperative we keep our home filled with the present of his Glory shinning all around us evert day, and night. God loves to spread his blessings in our homes. The blessings of the Lord are wonderful to feel in your heart. It is essential to walk every day in the love of Jesus in your hearts, and it will spread out in our communities.

The blessings God has filled in our home allows other individual's to be drawn to the arms of Jesus. "Ye are the light of the world. A city that set on an hill cannot be hid" (KJV). Example, it is just like a big two-story house sating on top of the hill, and it is surrounded by other houses with bright lights. You can see the house down the road, and before you get close to it.

God light should also shine bright in us, and it will light up on the inside and the outside. The people that are near us should recognize that God live in us, and in our home. It is a blessing God's light shines in our home to keep the over flowing love peeking through always.

God's Blessing Plans

God plans are the right comfort zone for us. It is imperative as a true disciple of God to keep your light shining bright, and we must be a light to the world. The light of God in your home should not have no darkness in it.

It is essential to keep Good first in our life always, and never let your light go dim in our home. A home filled with love can make someone else heart bubble with joy. The love that we show in our home can help someone else to follow that bright light, and find the right road to Jesus. Example, we can be in a mall walking, and talking to our family.

One day, I spoke, and smile at this young lady in the mall, and we started talking. The young lady told me, I am glad to have a good conservation with you today. It was a beautiful day, and the woman was going through sometimes in her life.

God's Blessing Plans

The lady told me there is a glow on your face. The woman paused for a few moments, and said you are a Christian woman. I replied to the young lady, and said yes. I shared with the young woman where I attended church. The next Sunday the lady came to my church service, and gave her life to Christ, and joined the church.

It is the light of God that shine in our life that draw people to Christ. "Let your light so shine before men, that they may see your good works, and glorify your Father which is in heaven" (KJV). It is imperative to be like a light to the people in the world to see the light of God in us, and to follow Jesus Christ.

Example it is like walking into a dark house, and no lights is on. You are bumping into everything trying to find the light switch. The light that is in us helps others to find their way to Christ. "But the path of the just is as a shining light, that shineth more, and more unto the prefect day" (KJV). It is imperative to have the love of Jesus in our home, and our hearts let it spread with the light of Jesus Christ. God's plan will never go wrong in our home, and life.

Walking in the blessing plans of God

It is blessing to serve God every day, and live a successful life. "In that I command thee this day to love the Lord thy God, to walk in his ways, and to keep his commandments, and his status and his judgements, that thou mayest live, and multiply: and the Lord" KJV). It is imperative we must do the things God required for us to do.

Sometimes the enemy will try to trick the people of God to walk in another direction in life. Why choice God's plans? The plans of God will hold a better future for us, and it comes with full benefits. There are no changes or clause in this benefit package while walking in the plans of God.

The plans of God are one hundred percent guarantee for a complete life time for us. The God, we serve today is awesome right by himself, and the Lord will take good care of us. "Be strong and of good courage, fear not, nor be afraid of them: for the Lord thy God, he is it doth go with thee, nor sake thee; he will not fail thee nor forsake thee" (KJV). God is right there beside of us, and there is no need to be frighten by anything going on around you.

When, we walk in the love of Jesus, and serve the Master according to his will the blessing able to overflow in our life. It is imperative to allow God to be the head in our life. God wanted Abram to go in another country to live, and not live around family during that season in his life.

God wanted Abram attention, and the Lord wanted Abram to be an awesome man of God in another land. "And I will make of thee a great nation, and I will bless thee, and make thy name great; and thou shalt be a blessing" (KJV). It is imperative for us to listen to the voice of God, and obey God's will for our life.

God's Blessing Plans

We must learn to follow the hands of God, and stay in
his will to receive the blessings of the Lord. Sometimes
God may want us to move from certain people, and listen to
the divine instruction from God to receive from the
Master's table.

"To everything there is a season, and a time for every
purpose under the heaven" (KJV). God already have the
plans for our life and the directions to follow to walk into
our blessings. "By faith Abraham, when he was called to go
out into a place which he should after receive for an
inheritance, obeyed; and he went out not knowing whither
he went" (KJV). The blessings God has promised to bless
us, and to take care of us even in the rough times in your
life.

Sometimes the enemy will try to send a distraction in our
life, and try to make you lose your blessings from God. The
hands of God are filled with many blessings for us to walk
in, and enjoy life. God able to take something that looks

like nothing in life, and blow his breath on it, and it becomes life in a hopeless situation. God is the King of King that desires to bless us, and follow his commandments. God was the beginning of Abraham's faith walked in his life. God spoke into Abraham life and to take a trip to another land.

Abraham believed voice he heard was God. "Now faith is the substance of things hoped for, the evidence of things not seen" (KJV). The voice of God was so clear to Abraham ears. Abraham could not see the instructions that was written before his eyes. Abraham knew without any doubts it was the voice of God speaking to follow his instructions.

Abraham had faith in his heart to believe God for his blessings. The man of God knew it was not a dream, and Abraham trusted God. "For we walk by faith, not by sight" (KJV). It should not matter how it looked in the nature ream. God is a great rewarder, able to bless us by walking in the presents of Lord by our faith.

"By faith Noah, being warned by God of things not seen as yet, moved with fear, prepared an ark to saving of his house; by which he commanded the world, and become an heir of the righteousness which is by faith" (KJV). Noah walked in the blessings by obeying God, and he did not turn away from the plans of God. Abraham acknowledge God, and begin to walk in the will of the Lord.

Abraham was chosen by God to follow his instruction, and persuasion from God about his faith trip would turn out. The steps that Abraham took, and follow the voice of God. We must first obey God, and keep all his commandment before us.

Abraham walked in the blessing of God, and his name became great among all the nations God did promise. God's plans are the best one for us. Yes, the people laughed, and made fun of Noah, and they thought he was crazy for building a big ark.

Noah did not stop doing what God asked him to do, and Noah kept preaching to the people. There was a reason for God allowing Noah to build this ark during that season. It is imperative to listen to what God wants us to do.

Noah love God, and wanted to continue his will no matter how silly it looked to anyone else. During, building the ark requested by God, Noah kept preaching the word of God to the people. The people refuse to listen to the servant of the Lord. "And the Lord said unto Noah, come thou and all thy house into the ark; for thee I have seen righteous before me in this generation" (KJV). Noah walked right in the blessing of the Lord. When, we do what God asked us to do for him a blessing is a waiting for us.

"And the rain was upon the earth forty days and forty nighty nights" (KJV). There was so much rain that came on the earth it destroyed a lot people because they refused to listen to the voice of God through Noah preaching the gospel of Jesus Christ. "But with thee will I establish my covenant; and thou shalt come into the ark, thou, and thy sons, and thy wife, and thy sons' wives with thee" (KJV). God had already promised Noah, and that he was going to bless Noah, and his family. God told Noah what animals to bring in the ark for that time. Noah obeys, God's plan and he was blessed by the hands of God.

Noah, and his family was saved through the flood sent on the earth. God had a covenant with Noah to keep his commandments, and he shall walk in the blessings of the Lord. It is essential for us to listen to the voice of the Lord, and walk in our blessings.

God's plans are the right one for us from the Masters hands. "Beloved, I wish above all things that thou mayest prosper and be in health, even as our soul prospereth" (KJV). It is the will of God for us to have good health, and live a joyful life to serve the Lord with happiness all the days of our life. God does not want us bound up, and living an unhappy life. It is imperative to understand God wants us to be free, bless, and doing the well in God. God plans is the right plans for our life.

Rejoicing in the blessing plans of God

It is essential for us to walk in the present of the Lord, and it gives us great joy lifting the name of Jesus. When we walk before a God that blesses us every day to wake up, and see another day no man not seen with their own eyes.

"God is able to make grace abound toward you; that ye, always having all sufficiency in all things, may abound to every good work" (KJV). It is imperative to trust God during your situation in life, and God able to take care of us. God wants us to be bless, and not showing no lack of anything in our life.

God's Blessing Plans

We must have high communication, and trust God with all the circumstances in our life. It is imperative for us to believe God every day, and never shift to the left or right. "But my God shall supply all your need according to his riches in glory by Christ Jesus" (KJV). God is letting us know don't worry I got you during your problems.

There may be a time in life you can't figure out the direction to go in life. It is essential that God understand the situate in your life. God wants us to totally depend on him in the midnight hour, and to stay in the path.

"But they that wait upon the Lord shall renew their strength; they shall mount up with wings as eagles; they shall run, and not be weary; and they shall walk, and not faint" (KJV). God wants us to wait on him to give us the directions to follow, and receive the blessing of the Lord.

God's eyes are in every place in the land, and the Lord knows our ups and down times in our life. God will lift us up like an eagle does her babies lift them up before they hit the ground, and get hurt. It is imperative to stay focus, and in the will of God to receive your blessings.

"And it shall come to pass, if thou shalt hearken diligently unto the voice of the LORD thy God, to observe and to do all his commandments which I command thee this day, that the LORD thy God will set thee on high above all nations of the earth" (KJV). The blessings will be sat before us, and doing what is required by the Lord.

The blessings of God will follow you, and continue to walk up right before the Lord. The God, we serve is bigger than man or woman hands. Example, we can walk into two department stores, and the shopping areas are designed totally different while trying to make your purchase. We shouldn't be trying to decide Jesus or the world. God's plan is the right choice 100% guarantee.

God's Blessing Plans

It is essential to understand for example, if an individual

is standing on the outside trying to climb in a window, and

trying to get in the house. The correct way to come in is

using the door, and it is the proper way. "Behold, I stand at

the door, and knock: if any man hears my voice, and open

the door, I will come in to him, and will sup with him, and

he be with me" (KJV). God don't want us to backup, and

miss our blessings by not following his commandments,

and serving the Lord.

God wants to bless us by staying on the right path, and

receive the right gift from God's hands. The best blessings

we can receive from God, and that is to serve the Lord with

our whole heart. "But as for me and my house, we will

serve the Lord" (KJV). The blessing will remain in our

homes long as we continue to stay in the will of God, and

listen to obey the Lord.

God plans is the right one to keep in our life. The hands

of the all Mighty God will never lose his power to give us

love, peace, and joy that wonderful blessing plans for our life. The greatest plans are from our Masters hands. Jesus is the answer today, and the Lord will always make away for us. Keeping God close in our life will bring love, peace & joy in our life.

.

God's Blessing Plans

www.ingramcontent.com/pod-product-compliance
Lightning Source LLC
Chambersburg PA
CBHW060357090426
42734CB00011B/2164